POINTING *to the* PROMISE

AN ADVENT STUDY GUIDE

Written by: Kayla Ferris

Copyright © 2020 by Proverbs 31 Ministries

All Scripture quotations are English Standard Version (ESV) unless otherwise noted.

*We must exchange
whispers with God
before shouts
with the world.*

LYSA TERKEURST

Pair your study guide with the First 5 mobile app!

This Study Guide is designed to accompany your study of Scripture in the First 5 mobile app. You can use it as a standalone study, or as an accompanying guide to the daily content within First 5.

First 5 is a free mobile app developed by Proverbs 31 Ministries to transform your daily time with God.

Go to the app store on your smartphone, download the First 5 app and create a free account!
WWW.FIRST5.ORG

Introduction

Over 2,000 years ago, a star appeared in the night sky. It made a group of sages wonder. It was unlike any star they had seen. In a culture steeped in astrology, their first question was *"What does it mean?"* That search for meaning led them on a life-changing quest to a town in Judea called Bethlehem, and to a little boy named Jesus.

Amazing, isn't it?! These "wise men" from the Christmas story were foreigners. Yet God met them exactly where they were. He utilized their interest in stars by creating one that would catch their attention. He planted in their ears Jewish stories and prophecies. He steered their attention toward Judea. He led them to a palace for more information. And then He allowed the star He created to physically navigate them to a small house where a young boy lived. Not just any boy. God's own Son.

Oh, how God delights in pointing us to His Son.

That is what you will see in this study. God pointing to His Son. It began thousands of years before Jesus was even born. God gave prophecies to His prophets and promises to His people. A Messiah was coming! A Savior would be born for you! Look for Him! Watch for Him! Such anticipation.

As the moment came closer, heaven started stirring. Angels began making appearances — to an old man in the temple, to a virgin woman in the middle of nowhere, to a heartbroken bachelor who was about to call off his engagement. Something was happening. Everything was pointing to the embryo that grew inside Mary. This Miracle caused an unborn baby to leap and a young woman to sing! The Word was becoming flesh.

And then the day came! Our Savior was born! As He was bundled up and laid in a manger, God sent His entire heavenly host to sing about it in a field full of shepherds who were … get this … caring for lambs awaiting a Passover slaughter. Even in His birth announcement, God points us to His plan: His Son, this precious baby, would grow up so He could become the ultimate Passover lamb. He was born, so He could die, that we might live.

Yes, God delights in pointing to His Son. And through this study, He longs to do the same. To help us fix our gaze in this busy time. To guide our hearts back toward their first love. To transform us by the renewing of our minds. To put our focus exactly where it belongs … on His Son.

Today, and every day, God whispers to each heart, "Hello my child. Guess what? *A Savior has been born to you.* I can't wait to show Him to you! Will you come and see?"

What is Advent?

Maybe "advent" is a word you have heard once before, or maybe it is a custom you practice every year. Either way, there is much we can learn by exploring the meaning and traditions that surround this simple word.

Advent is defined as "the arrival of a notable person, thing or event."

It comes from the Latin word *adventus*, which means "coming." Every year, Christians around the world use the days leading up to Christmas to celebrate the advent of Jesus. It is an expectant waiting and preparing for our Savior. It reminds us of the many years the Jews spent longing for the Messiah. Praise God that day came, and Jesus was born! It also reminds us of the waiting and preparing we do today, as we await the Second Coming of Jesus. Our Savior came first as a tiny baby in a humble manger. He will come again as a mighty warrior and King! But there is also another "coming" that we should remember as well. It is the arrival of Christ in our hearts as we accept His gift of salvation.

So, the meaning of Christmas advent is simple. **It is a celebration and anticipation of Jesus' arrival.** But the many traditions that have journeyed along with it are as diverse and beautiful as the people who make up the Church.

In A.D. 567, a group of monks fasted every day in December leading up to Christmas. This is thought to be the first official advent celebrated. Throughout history, evidence of advent at Christmas is found in writings and documents. Today, Western Christianity celebrates what we traditionally think of as advent, usually beginning four Sundays before Christmas. Meanwhile, Eastern Christianity celebrates the Nativity Fast, a 40-day fast leading up to Christmas.

Some old advent traditions have come and gone. At one time in England, they created an advent image, a box with two dolls inside, one for Mary and one for Jesus. They would walk house to house with the image and one would pay a halfpenny to see it. It was considered bad luck not to see the box before Christmas Eve. There was also an Italian tradition that the shepherds came to see Jesus while playing pipes, so every year, Italians would march into Rome being led by bagpipes.

In Germany, they would create wreaths and hang from them boxes or candles counting down to Christmas. It was from this tradition that many churches and homes have advent wreaths to this day.

Maybe you have seen advent calendars at the store. While modern culture now uses these to count down toward a day of family, food and yes, presents, the advent calendar was originally created to help us count down and anticipate the birth of Jesus. Advent calendars can be a fun and meaningful way to prepare our hearts and minds by anticipating the baby in a manger and why He came.

A common tradition in Christian churches today is the use of advent candles. An advent wreath will hold four candles around the outside and one candle in the middle. Of the outside candles, three will be purple (or royal blue in some cases, signifying seriousness and royalty) and one will be pink (signifying joy). Each Sunday, an outside candle is lit, with the pink candle specifically being lit on the third Sunday. The final candle in the middle is white and is lit on Christmas. There are as many different interpretations on the meaning and symbolism of the candles as there are churches! One of my favorites is a candle for faithfulness, hope, joy and love.

Maybe you have your own traditions. Maybe you have special ornaments you hang on a tree, or maybe you listen to advent songs like "O Come, O Come, Emmanuel" and "Come, Thou Long Expected Jesus." Whether you light candles, open a calendar, fast, pray, study or (why not?) — play bagpipes — let's use this time and season to focus our hearts and minds on the Coming. Our Savior arrived as a baby in the manger. He arrived in our hearts when we received Him. And He will arrive again one day soon. Celebrate that anticipation this season!

Where The Story Is Found

To learn about Jesus' time here on earth, we turn to the Gospels. The "Gospels" refer to the first four books of the New Testament (Matthew, Mark, Luke and John). These four books are accounts of Jesus' life written by four different men, giving us four distinct perspectives. Many of the stories are repeated between books. However, each book offers its own unique view.

The story of Jesus' birth is found in the books of Matthew and Luke. It is not mentioned in Mark or John. Mark begins his Gospel account with Jesus' baptism.

John mostly does as well, yet before he goes into the baptism, he opens with a beautiful introduction to Jesus. We will look at John 1:1-14 to start off our study (more on that in Day 1).

On the next page, we have provided a reading guide for you to use as you follow along on this journey. As you can see, we will jump between Matthew and Luke quite a bit to get a full view of Jesus' birth story. Having both accounts gives us an excellent insight into the complete story.

Let's look behind the scenes into the books we will be studying.

Matthew

Matthew, son of Alphaeus, was a Jewish tax collector. Fellow Jewish neighbors and relatives despised tax collectors because of their collaboration with the Roman government. Collectors also had a foul reputation for taking more money than required. In Matthew 9:9, Jesus passes Matthew's tax booth and says *"Follow me."* Matthew walked away from his booth to become one of the 12 disciples of Jesus. Matthew had a unique eye-witness account of the life and ministry of Jesus.

Scholars believe Matthew recorded his Gospel account around late A.D. 50 to early A.D. 60. It is believed to have been written to the church in Antioch of Syria, which had both Jewish and gentile Christians. Matthew's Gospel account was widely and rapidly circulated from there.

One important theme to notice from Matthew's book is the emphasis on Jesus as royal. Many times throughout Matthew, Jesus is referred to as "Son of David," both to indicate Jesus' royal lineage and to remind people of God's promise to establish David's throne forever. (2 Samuel 7:12-13) Matthew wanted his readers to know that Jesus Christ was the long-awaited King and Messiah.

Luke

Luke, on the other hand, led a very different life than Matthew. Luke was a physician by trade and a gentile by birth (gentile simply means "not Jewish"). Luke was also a friend and ministry colleague with Paul. (Colossians 4:14) While Luke's book is not a personal eye-witness account, it is seen as a reliable source partly because he traveled frequently with Paul.

Scholars believe Luke was written around A.D. 62. It was written to "Theophilus," an unknown man who undoubtedly had wealth and social standing. (Luke 1:3) It was also written with other gentile Christians like Theophilus in mind.

Many people had been taught about Jesus. But how could they know who this Jesus was for sure? Who could they believe? Luke gathered eye-witness testimonies, studied all accounts for some time and compiled an orderly description for one reason. (Luke 1:1-4) He wanted everyone to know, with certainty, who Jesus was and why He came.

John

Because we will spend Day 1 in John, let's take a quick look at what makes his Gospel account unique. John, son of Zebedee, was a fisherman when Jesus called him. (Matthew 4:21) This apostle of Jesus was also referred to as "the [disciple] whom Jesus loved" (John 20:2). The Gospel of John was probably the last of the gospel accounts to be written. Scholars estimate it was around A.D. 70. One very early Church theologian, Clement of Alexandria, called the book of John a "spiritual gospel." John's account clearly shows Jesus as both the Messiah and Son of God. He also emphasizes belief in Jesus to receive eternal life. (John 3:16)

Reading Guide &
Major Moments

WEEK 1 - PROMISES

Day 1 – John 1:1-14 – The Word (Jesus) was with God, was God, and became flesh.
Day 2 – Matthew 1:1-17 – Matthew recorded the genealogy of Jesus Christ, focusing on the line of Judah.
Day 3 – Luke 3:23-38 – Luke recorded the genealogy of Jesus, going back to Adam.
Day 4 – Luke 1:5-17 – An angel foretold the birth of John to his father, Zechariah.
Day 5 – Luke 1:18-25 – Zechariah doubted the angel Gabriel's message and was reprimanded.

WEEK 2 - RESPONSE

Day 6 – Luke 1:26-38 – Gabriel told the virgin Mary that she would miraculously conceive the Son of God.
Day 7 – Matthew 1:18-21 – An angel informed Joseph that Mary's conception was from the Holy Spirit.
Day 8 – Matthew 1:22-25 – The virgin birth of Jesus fulfilled Isaiah's prophecy of Immanuel.
Day 9 – Luke 1:39-41 – The unborn John leapt when Mary visited Elizabeth.
Day 10 – Luke 1:41-45 – Through the Holy Spirit, Elizabeth blessed Mary and the baby inside her.

WEEK 3 - FAITHFULNESS

Day 11 – Luke 1:46-49 – Mary's Song of Praise magnified God and demonstrated her humility.
Day 12 – Luke 1:50-53 – Mary's Song of Praise stated that God exalts the humble and scatters the proud.
Day 13 – Luke 1:54-56 – Mary's Song of Praise confirmed that God is faithful to His promises.
Day 14 – Luke 1:57-66 – Elizabeth and Zechariah had a baby and named him John.
Day 15 – Luke 1:67-80 – Zechariah prophesied that John would point to the One who saves.

Reading Guide & Major Moments

WEEK 4 - HOPE

Day 16 – Luke 2:1-5 – Joseph and Mary traveled to Bethlehem for a Roman government registration.
Day 17 – Luke 2:6-7 – Jesus Christ was born and laid in a manger.
Day 18 – Luke 2:8-14 – An angel announced Jesus' birth to nearby shepherds.
Day 19 – Luke 2:15-20 – The shepherds visited Jesus and spread the good news.
Day 20 – Luke 2:21 – He was given the name Jesus.

WEEK 5 - JOY

Day 21 – Luke 2:22-35 – Simeon recognized the infant Jesus as the Christ and gave a blessing.
Day 22 – Luke 2:36-39 – With Jesus in the temple, Anna gave thanks and prophesied.
Day 23 – Matthew 2:1-2 – The wise men came looking for the king of the Jews.
Day 24 – Matthew 2:3-8 – King Herod felt threatened by news of the born Messiah.
Day 25 – Matthew 2:9-10 – The star guided the wise men to Jesus.

WEEK 6 - LOVE

Day 26 – Matthew 2:11-12 – The wise men worshipped Jesus and brought Him gifts.
Day 27 – Matthew 2:13-15 – Jesus' family fled to Egypt, and like Israel's past, there would be a new exodus.
Day 28 – Matthew 2:16-18 – Herod killed children in Bethlehem, and like Israel's past, mothers wept for their children.
Day 29 – Matthew 2:19-23 – Jesus' family returned to Nazareth, and like Israel's prophets of the past, He would be rejected.
Day 30 – Luke 2:40 – Jesus grew up and had the grace of God upon Him.

week one

Promises

Every promise of God was completely fulfilled in Jesus Christ.

Day One

┌─ **major moment:** ─────────────────────────────────┐

   The Word (Jesus) was with God, was God, and became flesh.

└──┘

Our study starts with the three words: *"In the beginning ..."* (John 1:1). This was an intentional echo of the words in Genesis 1:1, which says *"In the beginning, God created ..."*

According to John 1:1-2, who was with God in the beginning? To understand who this is, look at verse 14. There we learn that He was *"the only ___Son___ from the Father, full of grace and truth."* To find another name to whom this is referring, see who brought grace and truth in John 1:17.

Use John 1:1 to fill in the blanks for important attributes of Jesus.

" ___In the beginning___ *was the Word, and the Word* ___was with God___ *, and the Word* ___was God___ *."* Describe what you think each of these might mean.

John 1:4 talks about *"life."* This specific word signifies both physical **and** spiritual life. How is Jesus the author of both physical and spiritual life?

Read John 1:4-5. *"Light"* was often used as a metaphor for **salvation**. What might *"darkness"* represent? How does John's use of *"life"* and *"light"* look like the Christmas story?

John 1:14 says *"And the Word became flesh and dwelt among us ..."* This one statement is one of the greatest and most astonishing mysteries of the Bible. We could not reach God, so God came down to us. Without ceasing to be God, **He became human.**

The phrase "dwelt among us" literally translates as "pitched his tent" or "tabernacled."

Read Exodus 40:34–35. What was Moses' reaction to the tabernacle and why?

This reaction was consistent for anyone in the Old Testament who even came close to the glory of God.

Yet what does John 1:14 say that John and others have seen?

Because of Jesus' birth, we, too, can come close to the Father. In fact, John 1:12 says that if we receive Jesus and believe in His name, we can become what? Write a short prayer thanking God for the gift of His presence.

"And the Word became flesh and dwelt among us..."

John 1:14

Day Two

> **major moment:**
>
> ## Matthew recorded the genealogy of Jesus Christ, focusing on the line of Judah.

Right from the beginning, Matthew established the purpose of writing his account.

What word comes after Jesus in Matthew 1:1 (and is also used in verses 16 and 17)?

This is not a last name. The Greek word "*Christos*" comes from a Hebrew word *msh* meaning "anointed one." (John 1:41) This is where the term "Messiah" comes from.

By repeating this word three times, what does Matthew want to make clear?

Let's first unpack the genealogy in Matthew by structure. Matthew points out his specific structure in Matthew 1:17 by mentioning three groups of 14. Hebrews practiced a system called *gematria* where numerical values were assigned to letters of the Hebrew alphabet. The name "David" in Hebrew (a three-letter word, because there are no vowels in ancient Hebrew) equaled the number 14 when added together.

When you count the number of generations in Matthew 1:2-6, what number is David listed?

David was an important part of the promised Messiah. Read 2 Samuel 7:12-13. What promise did God make to David?

Next, let's take a look at the inferred meaning of Matthew's account. It is important to know that not every descendant of the family line is listed. This means those that are listed are significant. In this time period, a genealogy served as a résumé. Like a résumé, it was presumed a person would leave off the less desirable aspects. Yet Matthew seems to do the opposite!

Women were almost never listed in ancient genealogy. How many are listed here? (Matthew 1:3, 5, 6, 16)

Also astonishing, in a culture that viewed outsiders as "unclean people," four of the women listed are not Jewish. Why might Matthew have included people of different ethnicities? (John 3:16)

Let's look even deeper into some of these names.

- Genesis 38:13-18 tells us **Judah** and **Tamar** committed incest.
- Joshua 6:25 tells us **Rahab** was a prostitute.
- 2 Samuel 12:9 tells us **David** was an adulterer and a murderer.
- 2 Chronicles 12:14 says that **Rehoboam** did evil in the sight of God, a phrase that will describe most of the kings listed in Matthew 1:7-11.

The point Matthew makes is clear: Jesus Christ came into this world from an extremely dysfunctional family. In his commentary *Exalting Jesus in Matthew,* David Platt says, "Jesus came not because of Israel's righteousness, but in spite of Israel's sinfulness ... Praise be to God that He delights in saving sinful, immoral outcasts!"

How does the dysfunction of Christ's genealogy remind us of Christ's mission on earth?

In his book *Hidden Christmas,* Tim Keller says, "Christmas is not simply about a birth but about a coming." God promised Abraham He would bless all nations. God promised David a forever kingdom. Yet it took **thousands of years** for God's promise to come about.

What does this tell you about God's timing?

What does Habakkuk 2:3 and 2 Peter 3:9 remind us?

Day Three

> **major moment:**
>
> Luke recorded the genealogy of Jesus, going back to Adam.

Yesterday we looked at Matthew's account of Jesus' genealogy, and today we will look at Luke's account. You will notice some major differences between the two accounts. What is going on here? Let's take a look.

The focus of Matthew's account is on Jesus' royal lineage. He wanted to emphasize Jesus as King. Matthew's account is also abbreviated.

Luke's account focuses on the physical line. This is a very traditional Jewish genealogy. His focus was to provide a public, legal record for the lineage of Jesus.

The two accounts help us to see exactly what each writer wanted to emphasize in his recording. Let's start by looking at what is the same. Both accounts bring the line of Jesus through two major people.

Who is the last name listed in Luke 3:31?

Who is the third name listed in Luke 3:34?

These names are also mentioned in Matthew's account. No matter how it was traced, Jesus Christ is the absolute fulfillment of the lineage requirements for the promised Messiah.

Now let's look at the difference between the two writers, Matthew and Luke. Look back at the "Where The Story Is Found" section of our guide.

What ethnicity was Matthew? With whom did Matthew begin Jesus' genealogy in Matthew 1:2?

What ethnicity was Luke?

Abraham is considered the father of the Jewish nation, which was Matthew's focus. However, Luke, a gentile, takes the family line of Jesus to Adam. Adam is considered the father of humanity.

What might Luke be telling his audience of gentiles by relating Jesus to Adam?
(For a hint, look up 1 John 2:2.)

Circle the last three words of Luke 3:38. Luke has taken us all the way back to the beginning of creation.

Remember on Day 1 when we studied John 1:1-4? Who was there at the beginning and created all things?

_____

Now circle the first word of Luke 3:23.

Knowing what we know from John, who is at the beginning and end of this genealogy in Luke?

_____

What does this remind us about both the beginning and end of all history and time, present and future? (Revelation 22:13)

_____

Day Four

LUKE 1:5-17

> **major moment:**
>
> An angel foretold the birth of John to his father, Zechariah.

In Luke 1:5, we are given the impressive religious pedigree of Zechariah and Elizabeth. However, even more impressive is verse 6.

What do we learn from this verse?

This phrase does not mean that Zechariah and Elizabeth were sinless. Even under the Old Testament law, we are told *"there is no one who does not sin"* (2 Chronicles 6:36). Instead, what this phrase means is that Zechariah and Elizabeth did their best to keep the laws of the Torah and the prophets. They were "good" people. And good things always happen to good people, right? Of course, we know that is not the case in life.

Matthew 1:7 begins with a painful statement. *"But they had no child ..."* The absence of children was seen as a reproach, as a sign of sin, in ancient Judaism. Even though they were "good people," Zechariah and Elizabeth had been dealt disgrace and shame from being barren. (Luke 1:25) The text also tells us they were *"advanced in years"* (Luke 1:7), so this is something they had endured for a lifetime. In his commentary *Exalting Jesus in Luke*, Thabiti Anyabwile says, "... the striking thing is that they handled a lifelong disappointment and social shame with righteousness and blamelessness before God. They served God even though they did not have what they wanted." What a beautiful example this couple lived.

In examining your own life, can you say you have remained faithful even through life's disappointments?

The angel appears to Zechariah and tells him he will have a son, to be named John. John was to be *"great before the Lord"* (Luke 1:15). He would be set apart.

According to Luke 1:15, what would John be filled with? When would he be filled? Meditate on that for a moment.

The last words the Jewish people had heard from God were written in Malachi 400 years prior to this moment. This means for 400 years, God had been silent.

What were the words written in Malachi 4:5-6?

Who fulfills this in Luke 1:13-17?

Underline the last part of Luke 1:17. What was John's great purpose?

Day Five

LUKE 1:18-25

---

major moment:

Zechariah doubted the angel Gabriel's message and was reprimanded.

After hearing the amazing promise given by the angel in Luke 1:13-17, Zechariah says to the angel *"How shall I know this?"* (Luke 1:18) What Zechariah was asking, or rather demanding, is a sign from God. Yet Zechariah already had two signs! He was given a direct visit (not a dream or a vision) from an angel, one that he could both see and hear. (Luke 1:12-13) What a sign! In addition to the angel, Zechariah also had the Scriptures to back the angel's words. He knew the story of Abraham in Genesis 17:17.

What had God already done through Abraham?

But even a visit from an angel that was backed up by Scripture wasn't enough for Zechariah. He wanted more. He wanted proof. Unbelief can sneak in to even the most *"righteous"* and *"blameless"* of believers. (Luke 1:6)

What is the definition of faith? (Hebrews 11:1)

One of the struggles for Zechariah was his focus on his problem or limitation.

What problem was Zechariah focused on? (Luke 1:18)

Thabiti Anyabwile uses an excellent word picture. He writes: "Did you know you can block out the noonday sun with a quarter? All you have to do is bring the quarter right up to your eye. We sometimes hold our problems and limitations to our eyes in that way, bringing them so close to our eyes we cannot see the great, glowing sun of God's promises and God's power."

In what ways, past or present, have you held your problems so close they blocked out God?

The unbelief of Zechariah led him to receive a sign, just like he had asked.

What did the angel say would happen to him in Luke 1:20?

In a figurative way, how does sneaky unbelief do the same thing to us?

weekend reflections + prayer

This week, we have talked about promises. In the beginning, God (and the Word) created the world. He created us in perfect relationship with Him. But sin messed up that relationship. There was no way for us as humans to find our way back to God. So, God promised Abraham He would send someone, a descendant, to bless the whole world. God promised David He would send someone, a descendant, to be a forever perfect King. And God did send someone. He sent Himself.

God, the Son, became flesh. He came down to be close to us once again, to restore the relationship that sin ruined.

Christmas reminds us that every promise of God was completely fulfilled in Jesus Christ.

God's promises are for you and me specifically. He promises fullness, forgiveness and fellowship with Him. He promises love, life and light that the darkness cannot overcome. And just like Zechariah, we all have a choice. Will we choose to believe and accept the promise God makes to us? Jesus is all the proof we need that God will always keep His promise.

prayer:

Dear God, thank You for Your promise to come back and save us. We couldn't do it ourselves, and we are lost without You. Thank You for the promises You made throughout history, and for allowing us to see them fulfilled in Jesus. You are true to Your Word. Strengthen my faith, that I might not forget Your faithfulness. In Jesus' name, amen.

week two

Response

Christmas requires us to respond.

Day Six

LUKE 1:26-38

---
major moment:

Gabriel told the virgin Mary that she would
miraculously conceive the Son of God.

Who gives Mary a special announcement in Luke 1:26?

_____

We saw this name previously with the message given to Zechariah.

What did we learn about this particular angel from Luke 1:19?

_____

There are many similarities between the announcement to Mary and to Zechariah. Both received
a visit from an angel, and both were startled. Both were commanded to not be afraid and told
they would have a son. Both knew this would normally be physically impossible.

Write the question Zechariah asks the angel in Luke 1:18.

Now write the question Mary asks in Luke 1:34.

Zechariah basically asks for proof while Mary asks "How will you do it?"
What is the main difference?

The birth announcement of Jesus found in Luke 1:31-35 holds within it many of the miraculous mysteries of God. We find the miracle of a virgin conception. We discover the incarnation, the idea that God will become fully human, while still fully God. We also uncover the truth of the Trinity, God as three persons in one essence: Father, Son and Holy Spirit.

These truths can still overwhelm our minds today. Yet what assurance did Gabriel give in Luke 1:37?

What does that mean to you?

Mary, a young teenager in a remote, forgotten little town, had found *"favor with God"* (Luke 1:30). When we read her response in Luke 1:38, we can understand why. The news from the angel was unparalleled, but it completely changed the trajectory of her life. Her future marriage, and therefore livelihood, were in jeopardy. Her social standing and credibility were ruined. This announcement would cost her every dream and plan she had made for her life. Yet Mary will go down in history as someone who responded to God with tremendous faith. Take a moment to fill in the faith responses of these other notable people. Then, in the spaces available, write what you observe about faith through this exercise.

Person of Faith	Scripture Reference	Repsonse
MARY	LUKE 1:38	*"Behold, I am the servant of the Lord; let it be to me according to your word."*
RUTH	RUTH 1:16	
ESTHER	ESTHER 4:16B	
JOB	JOB 13:15	
ISAIAH	ISAIAH 6:8	
JESUS	LUKE 22:42	

Day Seven

> **major moment:**
>
> ## An angel informed Joseph that Mary's conception was from the Holy Spirit.

Matthew 1:18-20 tells us twice that Mary's baby was *"from the Holy Spirit."* One of the foundational tenets of Christianity is the virgin birth of Jesus Christ. There are many who cannot get beyond the impossibility of such a phrasing as "virgin birth." Indeed, in human reasoning, it is impossible. Yet, let's look deeper into why such a truth is important to what we believe.

A vital aspect to understanding the Bible is to understand that Jesus Christ was God in flesh. (John 1:14) That means Jesus was both fully human and fully God. This is essential.

David Platt writes, "There are, after all, other ways Jesus could have come into the world." Platt gives two scenarios: If Jesus had come without any human parents, it would be hard to believe that He could relate to us. If Jesus had come from two biological parents, it would be hard to believe that He wasn't just like us. So God, in His perfect wisdom, designed a virgin birth.

Why is it important that Jesus be both fully human and fully God? Jesus had to be fully human because only a perfect, sinless death on our behalf could pay the price of our sin. Jesus had to be fully God because no human man could do this on his own. Only God could save us.

What are some of the ways Jesus showed He was human? (Matthew 4:2; 8:24; 26:36-39)

Why is that important? (Hint: Hebrews 2:17-18)

_____

What are some of the ways Jesus showed He was God? (Matthew 8:27; 9:1-6)

_____

Why is this important? (Hint: Hebrews 1:3; Titus 2:13-14)

_____

Next, let's take a look at the main character in today's reading, Joseph. Tim Keller writes, "Consider what the announcement of the angel meant to Joseph and Mary. ... They are going to be shamed, socially excluded and rejected. They are going to be second-class citizens forever. So the message is 'If Jesus Christ comes into your life, you are going to kiss your stellar reputation goodbye.' Joseph will see that having Jesus in his life means not just damage to his social standing but also danger to his very life. What is the application to us? If you want Jesus in your life, it is going to take bravery."

What do we know about Joseph's character in Matthew 1:19, 24?

Keller gives us several ways it takes courage to have Jesus in our lives: It takes courage to take the world's disdain of Christ; it takes courage to deny ourselves and our plans; wants, etc. and it takes courage to admit we are sinful. How do these relate to Jesus' adoptive father, Joseph, and to you as well?

"Behold, the virgin shall conceive and bear a son, and they shall call his name Immanuel, (which means, God with us)."

Matthew 1:23

Day Eight

---

major moment:

The virgin birth of Jesus fulfilled Isaiah's prophecy of Immanuel.

Matthew makes a point to show how the virgin birth of Jesus was a fulfillment of the Old Testament prophecies regarding the Messiah. Seven hundred years before Jesus was born, Isaiah wrote down the words in Isaiah 7:14.

What did Isaiah's prophecy say?

The Bible is full of Old Testament prophecies that Jesus perfectly fulfilled. God always, always, keeps His Word. He is always faithful in His promises.

How does knowing this give you confidence as you read verses like Deuteronomy 31:8, Psalm 46:1 or Revelation 21:4?

We learn from Matthew 1:21, 25 that Joseph was to name the baby "Jesus." The name Jesus means "Yahweh (the Lord) saves." It is a befitting name. Yet we learn from Matthew 1:23 that he was also to be "Immanuel."

Remember on Day 1 when we studied John 1:1-4? Who was there at the beginning and created all things?

What does the name "Immanuel" mean?

Sin separates us from God. This can be seen all the way back to the beginning, back in the Garden of Eden. But Jesus came to save us from sin. He restores our relationship with Him.

Replace the names in the following sentence with their meaning:

Because of JESUS, we have IMMANUEL.
_____

According to Matthew 28:20, how long will Jesus be "Immanuel"?
_____

Day Nine

---

major moment:

The unborn John leapt when Mary visited Elizabeth.

To provide some context, in the verses right before today's reading, we see that the angel Gabriel had visited Mary to tell her she would have a baby even though she was a virgin. This would not be just any child, but the *"Son of the Most High"* (Luke 1:32). In Luke 1:39, we learn that Mary then took a trip to visit Elizabeth.

According to Luke 1:39, when (or how) did Mary leave for this trip?

Copy the words of Psalm 119:60. Does this reflect your life?

Today we are going to focus specifically on John's reaction to the announcement of Jesus.

How old was John when he first encountered Jesus? How old was Jesus? Yes, this is a "trick question," but one with a valid point. (Luke 1:39-42)

Thabiti Anyabwile says, "Luke does not begin his Gospel with a full-grown Jesus or even with an infant Jesus. Luke begins his Gospel in the wombs of two women. In doing so, Luke tells us about the dignity and importance of pregnancy and children. He illustrates how God in infinite wisdom placed the weight of his entire plan of redemption on the back of an unborn baby." Thabiti Anyabwile entitled this section *"Jesus was a Fetus."*

What does this passage teach us about life's beginning?

Luke 1:41 says that when Elizabeth heard Mary's greeting, the baby John *"leaped in her womb."* How is this possible? Let's remember what we learned about John from his father Zechariah's encounter with the angel.

Luke 1:15 says that even from his mother's womb, John would have what?

Luke 1:17 says that John's job would be to make ready for the Lord, what?

John has begun his prophetic role of being the forerunner to the Messiah, of making a way for the Christ ... **even from within the womb** of his mother.

After John leaps for joy, what happens to his mother Elizabeth? (Luke 1:41)

Day Ten

┌─ major moment: ─────────────────────────────────┐

Through the Holy Spirit, Elizabeth blessed
Mary and the baby inside her.

└───┘

Yesterday we focused on the reaction of the unborn child, John. Today let's focus on the reaction of his elderly mother, Elizabeth. Elizabeth did not need to be told of Mary's pregnancy or of the child she carried. Elizabeth calls the baby inside Mary *"my Lord"* (Luke 1:43).

What did Luke 1:41 teach us about Elizabeth?

What does 1 Corinthians 12:3 teach us about calling Jesus *"Lord"*?

When the Holy Spirit revealed Jesus to her, Elizabeth reacted.

Fill in the blank.

"and she _____ with a _____ _____ ..."

Do our lives announce Jesus' presence in such a way? How could we improve on that?

Elizabeth's reaction involves a blessing, not just on Mary, but also to Mary's child. In fact, it is Mary's role as *"mother"* (v. 43) that caused her to be blessed *"among women"* (v. 42). And we learned that becoming a mother was not from Mary's doing. Indeed, it is not on her own merit that Mary is blessed, but rather, she is blessed because of the son inside of her.

Read 2 Timothy 1:9. How is that also true of us?

It can also be said that through the Holy Spirit, Elizabeth presents us with the very first "beatitude." A beatitude is a "blessed are…" statement. Jesus gave us many beatitudes in His Sermon on the Mount.

Look at the beatitudes Jesus gave in Luke 6:20-23. Jot down your thoughts.

_____

Fill in the beatitude from Luke 1:45 with a single word.

_____

"Blessed is she who _____ ."

weekend reflections + prayer

One theme for this week has been "response." An angel came to Mary and Joseph to deliver the Good News. The Holy Spirit revealed the Good News to John and Elizabeth as well. A baby was to be born. It would be miraculous, a virgin birth. He would be the one the prophets foresaw. This child would be God's own Son. And He would save His people from their sins.

Mary responded to the message with inspiring faithfulness. Joseph responded in quiet obedience. The prophets of the past had responded with a hopeful anticipation. The yet-born John responded by leaping for joy. The elderly Elizabeth responded by shouting blessings. Men, women, young, old, past, present and yes, even us in the future … all are presented with the Good News of Christmas. And **Christmas requires of us a response.**

Will we allow the message to change us? Will it inspire us to faithfulness and obedience? Will it encourage us toward hope and joy? Jesus said, "*What you hear whispered, proclaim on the housetops*" (Matthew 10:27). Will we shout it from the rooftops?! Let us go out this season with lives that shout "JOY to the world, our Lord has come! Let earth receive her King."

> **prayer:**
>
> *Father, thank You for the Good News of Christmas. And thank You for examples of godly response. Help me to be faithful and obedient. Help me see the joy found in You. Help me to live a life that shouts Your goodness and glory. In Jesus' name, amen.*

week three

Faithfulness

Jesus is the proof that our God is faithful.

Day Eleven

LUKE 1:46-49

┌─ **major moment:** ─────────────────────────────────┐

Mary's Song of Praise magnified God and demonstrated her humility.

└──┘

Mary's Song of Praise in Luke 1:46–55 is also referred to as the *Magnificat*. This is a term translated from a Latin word meaning "to magnify" or "to enlarge."

Who does Mary "magnify" in verses 46-49?

_____

In Luke 1:47, Mary refers to God as *"my Savior."*

What kind of person is in need of a Savior?

_____

What do these two points teach us about Mary?

_____

In many ways, Mary's Song of Praise is similar to Hannah's song found in 1 Samuel 2.
But before Hannah wrote her praise song, she offered another prayer before the Lord.

Read 1 Samuel 1:11. What does Hannah call herself that Mary also calls herself in Luke 1:48?
What do you think this term means?

_____

Fill in the blanks from Luke 1:49.

_____

"for he who is _____ *has* _____ _____
_____ *for me, and* _____ *is his name."*

What do we learn about God from this verse?

This first section of Mary's song is full of amazement that God would choose **her.** I love this quote from Tim Keller: "Every Christian is like Mary. Everyone who puts faith in Christ receives, by the Holy Spirit, *'Christ in you, the hope of glory'* (Colossians 1:27). We should be just as shocked that God would give us — with all our smallness and flaws — such a mighty gift."

Compose your own words to the Lord expressing your amazement that *"Jesus Christ is in you"* (2 Corinthians 13:5) and that He chose **you** for such a gift.

Day Twelve

---
major moment:

Mary's Song of Praise stated that God exalts the humble and scatters the proud.

The next section of Mary's Song of Praise highlights the fact that God's ways are often the opposite of the world's ways. Just as God's grand plan of salvation would surprisingly begin with a young girl from a "nowhere" town, God's ways are often not what we might expect. And if God's plan and *"mercy is for those who fear him"* (Luke 1:50), then what does it look like to live this way? (Also, what doesn't it look like?!) Let's take a look.

Luke 1:51 says he has scattered "the proud." What does Proverbs 16:18 say about the proud?

Luke 1:52 talks about *"the mighty."* What does Psalm 73:26 say about human strength?

Luke 1:53 speaks to *"the rich."* What does Jesus say in Luke 6:24 say about the rich? (It is important to remember that *"the rich"* is less about a physical bank account and more about a spiritual attitude. We all have a tendency to believe we have a "spiritual bank account" where our good deeds make deposits and our sins make withdrawals. This attitude can make us think we are "rich" in our own righteousness and works. Additionally, Proverbs 10:15 says, *"A rich man's wealth is his strong city ..."* Why is this wrong? Because if God is not our strong city, but our wealth is, who needs Him? And if we are rich in our own works, then who needs Jesus?! Oh, what a dangerous place to be!

According to Luke 1:50-53, **living in a prideful, mighty, "rich in self" attitude leaves us scattered, fallen and empty.**

How have you seen this to be true?

Now let's take a look at the opposite of these words.

The opposite of *"the proud"* are *"those of humble estate"* (Luke 1:52).
What does Job 5:11 say about humility?

The opposite of *"the mighty"* is *"the strength of [God's] arm"* (Luke 1:51). When is God's strength made perfect according to 2 Corinthians 12:9? What does Isaiah 40:29 say about our weakness?

The opposite of *"the rich"* are *"the hungry"* (Luke 1:53). What does Psalm 107:9 say about being hungry?

According to Luke 1:50-53, when we are humble, weak and hungry for God, then we will be lifted up, given strength and filled with good things.

How have you seen this to be true?

Day Thirteen

---

major moment:

Mary's Song of Praise confirmed that God is faithful to His promises.

Mary ends her song by praising God for His faithfulness. Many, many years before, God had made a promise to Abraham, the father of the nation of Israel. Mary knew this child she carried was to be the fulfillment of that promise. Let's take a look today at Abraham.

Abraham (who was called "Abram" before God renamed him) received a message from God.

What promise did God give to Abraham in Genesis 12:2-3?

How are all the families of the earth blessed through Jesus' birth?

God gave Abraham a promise that He would fulfill nearly 2,000 years later. But this is not all that God told Abraham in this moment.

Go back and read Genesis 12:1. What did God ask of Abraham?

Hebrews 11:8 also talks about this moment. What additional information do we learn from this verse?

In looking at Mary's song reference to Abraham, Tim Keller wrote: "Anybody who wants to become a Christian must basically do the same thing as Mary and Abraham before her. Becoming a Christian is not like signing up for a gym; it is not a 'living well' program that will help you flourish and realize your potential. ... Christian faith is not a negotiation but a surrender. **It means to take your hands off your life**" (Emphasis added).

How was this true for Mary and Abraham? And is it true of you? How so?

Mary ends her song with the word *"forever."* This word also means "for eternity." Luke 1:55 tells us that the promise of God was for Abraham **and his offspring**, for eternity.

What does Galatians 3:29 say about the offspring of Abraham?

God promised to bless the entire world through the offspring of Abraham. He fulfilled that promise through Jesus Christ. Now those of us who are in Christ are considered offspring of Abraham as well. Knowing that Christ lives inside us, and we are children of God, should fill us with overflowing hope that spills over and blesses the world.

How can you be a blessing today?

Day Fourteen

---
major moment:

Elizabeth and Zechariah had a baby and named him John.

In today's reading, Luke walks us through the birth of John. Let's refresh our memories on three aspects of Zechariah's encounter with the angel nine months earlier.

Luke 1:13 – What did the angel tell Zechariah to name the baby?

Luke 1:14 says *"you will have joy and gladness and ..."* what?

Luke 1:20 – What happened to Zechariah because of his unbelief?

We are going to look at how each of these plays out in today's reading in Luke 1:57-66. We will start with John's **name**. Naming rights in this time and culture belonged to the father. Naming a child showed a parent's authority. The Bible lays out good guidelines for the relationship between parents and children.

> Read Proverbs 1:8 (Old Testament) and Colossians 3:20 (New Testament). What should the relationship between child and parent look like?

However, in today's story, the naming ceremony does not go as expected. Elizabeth and Zechariah both confirmed that their baby would not be given the family name. Zechariah gave up his right to name his child, and instead obeyed God's message to name him "John." In turn, it was a reminder that John's ultimate job was not to obey Zechariah. John was to obey **God's authority** over his life.

> While it is important for young people to respect their elders, who is it even more important that they submit to and obey?

Next, let's look at the second aspect of the angel's message to Zechariah. It was foretold that *"many will rejoice"* at John's birth.

> According to Luke 1:58-59, who is with Elizabeth after the birth? And according to verse 58, what do they do?

What does Hebrews 10:24-25 remind us about the importance of community?

Finally, let's look at Zechariah's condition. Luke 1:20 says he was unable to speak. Because verse 62 mentions the people making signs to Zechariah, we can also assume he was deaf as well. For nine months, Zechariah has not heard a sound. He has not spoken a word.

According to Luke 1:64, what is the first thing Zechariah speaks?

In his commentary on Luke in the *Expository Thoughts on the Gospels,* J.C. Ryle wrote, "Let us take heed that affliction does us good, as it did to Zecharias. ... 'Sanctified afflictions' are 'spiritual promotions.' The sorrow that humbles us, and drives us nearer to God, is a blessing, and a downright gain."

How was affliction perhaps a blessing for Zechariah? How have you seen this to be true for you or someone you love?

Day Fifteen

LUKE 1:67-80

---

major moment:

Zechariah prophesied that John would point to the one who saves.

Zechariah's prophecy is often referred to as the Benedictus. This comes from the Latin form of the first word Zechariah spoke, which is *"Blessed"* (Luke 1:68). It means to praise or to be worthy of honor.

According to Luke 1:68, why does Zechariah say God is to be "blessed" or praised?

Zechariah was a man who understood the power of restoration. Zechariah had made a mistake. He had questioned God's messenger in an attitude of complete unbelief. But … Zechariah's mistake did not mean an end to his ministry! Now this priest is in a position to prophesy.

Can you think of other biblical figures who made mistakes, but God still used to further His plans and Kingdom? (If you need an example, read about Peter in Luke 22:54-62.)

Do you believe God can still use people who make mistakes today?
(Hint, the answer is yes!)

Zechariah's words begin and end (Luke 1:69, 79) with similar metaphors from Psalm 132:17, which says, *"There I will make a horn to sprout for David; I have prepared a lamp for my anointed."* A horn was seen as an animal's strength and was a symbol of power. A lamp brought light, a symbol of goodness, truth and clarity.

How is Jesus both the "horn" and the "light" of salvation?

Zechariah mentions David (v. 69) and the prophets of old (v. 70). He talks about *"our fathers,"* specifically *"father Abraham"* (Luke 1:72-73). All of the messages and promises given to Abraham, David, the prophets and others were all about to converge at this very moment in time. Everything was about to be fulfilled with the coming salvation of the Messiah.

What does this tell us about the purpose of the Old Testament? Who does it **all** point toward?

Zechariah knows his son, John, is not the promised Messiah. But he also knows John will play an important part.

How does Luke 1:76 compare to Malachi 3:1?

How does Luke 1:80 compare to Isaiah 40:3?

weekend reflections + prayer

Have you noticed the fingerprints of God's faithfulness throughout this week's passages? Mary knew God promised to be with the humble and the weak. Yet she was still amazed by God's faithfulness to bring about His promise through her. Zechariah had found it hard to believe that God could deliver on the promise that was made to him, and it had cost him. Yet when his son was born, Zechariah's mouth opened in praise.

Both Mary and Zechariah had remembered the stories from old. Stories about promises to Abraham, to David, and to the prophets. But can you imagine what it must have been like to be living in the very moment when all of those promises came true? This, friends, is the beauty of Christmas. **Christmas is the proof that our God is faithful.**

God was faithful to His promises of old. He was faithful to Mary and Zechariah. And God will be faithful to us as well. So guess what? If God calls you His child, you are. (1 John 3:1) If He says He cares for you (1 Peter 5:7), it is because He does. It also means that if God says one day there will be *"no more death or mourning or crying or pain …"* (Revelation 21:4), then you can **know**, with 100 percent certainty, that this day is coming soon! Amen. Come, Lord Jesus!

If God said it, He meant it. If God promised it, He will do it. Christmas proves our God is faithful.

> **prayer:**
>
> *Father God, You are faithful and true. Your Word always comes to pass. The life of Jesus is proof that You always keep Your promises. I confess, Lord, that I do not always understand Your timing. But I recommit myself to trusting You. In Jesus' name, amen.*

week four

Hope

Because Jesus was born and laid
in a manger, we have hope.

Day Sixteen

LUKE 2:1-5

> **major moment:**
>
> ## Joseph and Mary traveled to Bethlehem for a Roman government registration.

In today's reading, Luke wants to establish a historical context and explanation for the birth of Jesus. Let's dive into a little Roman history. Luke 2:1 mentions *"Caesar Augustus."* This leader was born with the name Gaius Octavius in September of 63 B.C. Octavius was actually the great nephew of Julius Caesar. The Roman senate gave him the honorary name of Caesar Augustus and named him ruler in 27 B.C. As a leader, he was harsh and unrelenting, yet he was best known for having an organized and peaceful reign.

What did this Roman emperor issue in Luke 2:1?

It was fairly common for people to return to their family towns to register with the Roman government. There are records out of Egypt from this time period that tell of this happening as well.

According to Luke 2:4, where did the Roman edict cause Joseph to travel?

What does Micah 5:2 say about the promised Messiah?

_____

What does Isaiah 11:1 say about the promised Messiah?

_____

Luke calls Bethlehem the "*city of David*." Read 1 Samuel 17:12. This verse says that David is the son of who … from where …?

_____

In his commentary on Luke, Darrell L. Bock writes, "... the mention of the census explains how a couple from Nazareth gave birth to a child in Bethlehem. The accidental events of history have become acts of destiny. Little actions have great significance, for the ruler was to come out of Bethlehem and only a governmental decree puts the parents in the right place." God used a Roman emperor and a registration of *"all the world"* (Luke 2:1) just to get Mary and Joseph to the right place at the right time.

What does this teach us about God?

One last interesting note. Many scholars wonder why Mary traveled to Bethlehem at all. Women were often not required to register. Luke also points out that Mary and Joseph were still "betrothed" (Luke 2:5) and not yet officially married. Some scholars speculate that perhaps Joseph was trying to take Mary out from under the harsh gossip and treatment of their hometown neighbors as she neared the end of her pregnancy. If this was the case, then even the painful treatment from others was used to bring about the good of God's great plan.

What does this teach us about the difficult situations we endure?

Day Seventeen

major moment:

Jesus Christ was born and laid in a manger.

Luke 2:6-7 are arguably two of the most understated verses in the Bible. Without much fanfare, Luke tells us that Mary *"gave birth to her firstborn son."* Such a simple line. Such extraordinary consequences. Before we dive into these two verses, let's look at a complementary verse in Isaiah.

Fill in the words from Isaiah 9:6:

"*For to us ____   _____ is _____,*

to _____ a son is _____."

To whom was the child born?

Tim Keller writes, *"… 'to us a son is given.'* It's a gift. It can be yours only if you are willing to receive it as a gift of grace.'" How is the birth of Jesus the best gift you could give or receive this year?

The fulfillment of Isaiah 9:6 happens in Luke 2:6-7. The time had come for Jesus to be born. What do we know of this event? Well, because we have the word *"manger"* or *"feeding trough,"* we know there were probably animals nearby. We often imagine this was a stable or barn. However, poor families often used the bottom story of their homes to bring in their animals at night, so it could have been a room. It could have been a cave. It also could have been an open courtyard. But let's focus on what we do know by taking a look at verse 7...

Where was baby Jesus placed?

Why were Joseph and Mary in this situation?

Have you ever been in a situation where there was no place for you? You feel like you don't belong? This is exactly where Jesus started his life ... in a manger, because there wasn't a place for him.

Read Luke 9:58. Did this ever change for Jesus?

How does Jesus' situation and His words in John 15:19 comfort us?

Christ Jesus came in the humblest of ways. The God of the universe, Creator of all, was born. And He was laid in a feed trough because there wasn't room for Him. How this thought ought to humble our hearts and rearrange our priorities! Matthew Henry once said, "But when we by faith view the Son of God being made man and lying in a manger, our vanity, ambition, and envy are checked. We cannot, with this object rightly before us, seek great things for ourselves or our children."

How does seeing God in a manger check your heart?

Old Testament Prophecies Fulfilled by Jesus' Birth

Since the fall, God has longed to again be close to the people He created. He had a plan in place: A Messiah would come. He would save God's people and restore the relationship. Yet how would we know when He arrived? Was it really the Messiah? Or just an imposter?

Thankfully, God left us many clues within the Old Testament so we could know the Messiah when He came. Note that these prophecies of the Messiah span from many prophets over many years.

ONE DAY, A CHILD WOULD BE BORN.

In Isaiah 9:6 it says, *"For to us a child is born, to us a son is given."*

This child would meet several requirements.

FIRST, HE WOULD BE FROM THE LINE OF DAVID.

In 2 Samuel 7:12-13, God promises David, *"I will raise up your offspring after you, who shall come from **your body**, and I will establish his kingdom. ... I will establish the throne of his kingdom forever."*

Jeremiah 23:5 reiterates, *"'Behold, the days are coming, declares the Lord, when I will raise up for David a righteous Branch, and he shall reign as king and deal wisely, and shall execute justice and righteousness in the land.'"*

SECOND, HE WOULD BE BORN IN BETHLEHEM.

Micah 5:2 specifically says, *"But you, O Bethlehem Ephrathah, who are too little to be among the clans of Judah, from you shall come forth for me one who is to be ruler in Israel, whose coming forth is from of old, from ancient days."*

THIRD, HE WOULD BE BORN TO A VIRGIN, BEGOTTEN NOT BY MAN, BUT BY GOD.

Isaiah 7:14 says, *"Therefore the Lord himself will give you a sign. Behold, the virgin shall conceive and bear a son, and shall call his name Immanuel."*

The Messianic psalm in Psalm 2:7 says, *"I will tell of the decree: The LORD said to me, "You are my Son; today I have begotten you."*

GOD ALSO TOLD OF A FORERUNNER TO THE MESSIAH.

Malachi 3:1 says, *"Behold, I send my messenger, and he will prepare the way before me. And the Lord whom you seek will suddenly come to his temple; and the messenger of the covenant in whom you delight, behold, he is coming, says the LORD of hosts."*

In Isaiah 40:3 it says, *"A voice cries: 'In the wilderness prepare the way of the LORD; make straight in the desert a highway for our God.'"*

WE KNOW THAT MEN WOULD COME SEEKING HIM FROM MANY NATIONS, BRINGING GIFTS.

Psalm 72:10-11 tells us, *"May the kings of Tarshish and of the coastlands render him tribute; may the kings of Sheba and Seba bring gifts! May all kings fall down before him, all nations serve him!"*

And Isaiah 60:6 says, *"A multitude of camels shall cover you, the young camels of Midian and Ephah; all those from Sheba shall come. They shall bring gold and frankincense, and shall bring good news, the praises of the Lord."*

BUT NOT ALL WOULD HONOR HIM. IN FACT, SOME KINGS WOULD PLOT TO KILL HIM.

Psalm 2:2 warns that *"The kings of the earth set themselves, and the rulers take counsel together, against the Lord and against his Anointed …"*

GOD ALSO SAYS THAT HIS SON WOULD COME OUT OF EGYPT, JUST LIKE ISRAEL DID IN THE PAST.

Hosea 11:1 says, *"When Israel was a child, I loved him, and out of Egypt I called my son."*

WE ALSO KNOW THAT THE MESSIAH WOULD BE LOOKED DOWN ON..

Isaiah 53:2-3 says it plainly, *"… he had no form or majesty that we should look at him, and no beauty that we should desire him. He was despised and rejected by men, a man of sorrows and acquainted with grief; and as one from whom men hide their faces he was despised, and we esteemed him not."*

WHAT IS ABSOLUTELY ASTOUNDING IS THAT THE BIRTH OF JESUS CHRIST PERFECTLY FULFILLED EVERY PROPHECY!

Jesus was miraculously born of a virgin, in the city of Bethlehem, because His "parents" were from the line of David. Another baby was born before Him, though. This baby was named John, and he would live in the wilderness and go before the Messiah to make the way. Wise men would come from far away, bringing gifts of gold and frankincense. But not everyone would be happy. King Herod felt threatened and plotted to kill Jesus, even as a baby. But Jesus' parents would run to Egypt for safety. And when the coast was clear, just like the Word said, God's Son would come out of Egypt. Then, they would settle in the lowly, despised village of Nazareth.

BECAUSE JESUS FULFILLED EVERY ONE OF THESE PROPHECIES, WE CAN KNOW THAT JESUS IS THE MESSIAH.

Do we see the beauty in that? We don't just have to wonder or hope. We can **know.** Jesus **IS** the Messiah. He is the One who came to restore our relationship with God. He is God's rescue plan. And He is worthy of all of our trust and devotion.

Day Eighteen

┌─ **major moment:** ─────────────────────────────────┐

An angel announced Jesus' birth to nearby shepherds.

└──┘

Shepherds sometimes had a bad reputation. Their work made them "unclean" for religious ceremonies, which were a vital part of the Jewish community. According to Thabiti Anyabwile, "they were considered unreliable and could not give testimony in the law courts. They were a despised class of people." Yet they received the first proclamation of Jesus' birth. They were not despised by God. Let's look at some other notable shepherds.

Who was a shepherd in Exodus 3:1?

Who was a shepherd in 1 Samuel 17:34?

Who is called a shepherd in Psalm 23?

Who called Himself a shepherd in John 10:11?

Scholars have studied the area around Bethlehem in context with the culture of the day. It is quite possible that these shepherds were located in a field about two miles from town and were responsible for caring for the sheep that were destined for the Passover sacrifice at the temple in a few months.

What did John the baptizer say to Jesus in John 1:29?

What does 1 Corinthians 5:7 say about Jesus?

In his message to the shepherds, the angel makes a bold proclamation. Luke 2:11 calls this baby *"a Savior, who is Christ the Lord."* The word *Christ* is a Greek word meaning "Anointed One." In Hebrew, this word is **"Messiah."** The word "Lord" is a translation of the name Yahweh or Jehovah. It refers only to **God** Himself.

In calling Jesus *"Christ the Lord,"* what is the angel saying?

Many times at Christmas, the phrase "peace on earth" is used. This expression comes from the multitude of angels praising God in Luke 2:14. Let's look a little deeper into this peace.

In verse 14, it says *"and on earth peace among"* whom?

The peace the angels declare is not an absence of conflict on earth among people. This word "peace" refers to a peace between God and people. It is a restoration of our relationship with God, which was severed by sin.

What does Jesus say about peace in John 16:33?

When we have peace with God, what should we then strive for, according to Romans 12:18?

Day Nineteen

> **major moment:**
>
> The shepherds visited Jesus and spread the good news.

As soon as the angels departed, the shepherds left to find the baby *"lying in the manger"* (Luke 2:16). And they found him exactly as the angel had told them. Can you just picture them, walking up to the manger and looking into the face of the newborn baby? Can you hear them excitedly telling Mary and Joseph about the multitude of angels? Maybe Mary and Joseph shared their experiences with angels as well. I can just hear a shepherd saying "I was so afraid, but the angel told me 'Fear not...'" and Mary and Joseph say "Yes! He said the same to us!" What we do know is that their experience together changed them. Let's look at how it affected both the shepherds and Mary.

What do the shepherds do in Luke 2:17 after seeing Jesus?

Many scholars consider the shepherds to be the first evangelists. They saw the Word of God fulfilled and went out to tell everyone they could. Darrell Bock says it this way: "When God's Word comes to pass, testimony should follow."

How have you seen God's Word come to pass in your own life? Read Luke 8:39.
How does this man, along with the shepherds, inspire you to share God with others?

When the shepherds shared their story, everyone who heard it "wondered" at what was told them. (Luke 2:18) This word means they were "amazed." They found it curious and interesting. But then they moved on. Let's look at Mary's response in contrast.

Fill in Luke 2:19

"But Mary _____ up all these

things, _____ them in her heart."

To "ponder" means to think seriously, to put thoughts together in an understandable way, to connect, to put into context. This is the way Mary "ponders" what she has heard. It is the way we should read and study God's Word as well.

What word does Psalm 119:130 use to describe the way God's Word brings light? When something is folded, it is compact. You can only see a part of the whole. How might we "unfold" God's Word?

To "treasure" means to keep it close. Here the word specifically means an **ongoing** thought process. It means to constantly remind ourselves of the truth and value and awe of what we learn. It is an attitude of the heart.

Tim Keller writes: "If you don't do both of these things – ponder and treasure the Word of God – you will not truly hear the message. Your ears will hear it but not your mind and heart. It won't sink in, comfort, convict, or change you."

What does Job 23:12 and Psalm 119:18 teach us about treasuring God's Word?

Day Twenty

---

major moment:

He was given the name Jesus.

Today we will see the faithfulness of Jesus' parents and the significance of His name by looking at many verses throughout the Bible. Let's start with His parents.

What law was given to the Jewish people in Genesis 17:11-12?

What did the angel tell Joseph specifically in Matthew 1:21?

What did the angel tell Mary specifically in Luke 1:31?

What does today's Scripture in Luke 2:21 say about Jesus' parents?

Mary and Joseph obeyed God's Word and direction. We often think of parenting as teaching obedience. But why is being obedient as a parent important?

The baby is given the name **"Jesus."** *"Jesus"* means "the Lord saves."

What did the angel say Jesus would save us from in Matthew 1:21?

According to 1 Peter 2:24, how did He do this?

The name "Jesus" is a translation of the Greek word *lēsous*. The equivalent to this word in Hebrew would be *Yeshua* or "Joshua."

What was the job of the Old Testament Joshua? Where was he to lead the people? (Joshua 1:1)

Read 1 Thessalonians 4:16-18 and Revelation 21:1-7. Where will Jesus lead His people?

weekend reflections + prayer

Rick Warren once said, "What gives me the most hope every day is God's grace; knowing that his grace is going to give me the strength for whatever I face, knowing that nothing is a surprise to God." This is the kind of hope that has permeated the passages this week.

Joseph traveled to Bethlehem because a Roman emperor told him to. Or so he thought. Why was there no room to be found for Mary? Why did our Savior have to be laid in a feeding trough for a bed? Then the first to hear the news that a Savior was born were *lowly, dirty shepherds*. All of this looks like disappointment.

BUT … these shepherds pronounce praise and Mary ponders! Why? Because the baby Jesus being born this very way means hope for this world. Yes, **Christmas is our reminder that because Jesus was born and was laid in a feeding trough, we can have hope.**

Under all of the worldly troubles we face, something bigger is working. What looks like disappointments could be the very workings of HOPE in our lives. God is on the throne. Nothing surprises Him. He never leaves our side. And these earthly troubles we face are preparing for us an eternal glory that will far outweigh them all. (2 Corinthians 4:17)

In every moment of every day, no matter what is going on around us, God is still in control. He was in control 2,000 years ago when Joseph was forced to travel to Bethlehem and Jesus was born with the animals and lowly shepherds came to visit. He offers that same hope to us today. No matter what your circumstances look like around you, His Hope can live inside you.

prayer:

God, we proclaim today that YOU are omnipotent. You are all powerful and unstoppable. Nothing can thwart Your plans. You are on the throne. Thank You for this clear reminder from the day Your Son was born. Help me to remember this when my circumstances feel hard and disappointing. Stir up Your hope inside me. In Jesus' name, amen.

week five

Joy

Joy is only found in Jesus.

Day Twenty-One

LUKE 2:22-35

---

major moment:

Simeon recognized the infant Jesus as the Christ and gave a blessing.

Today's reading opens with Mary and Joseph following the Jewish customs established in Leviticus. After the circumcision, there was a period of 33 days where the mother was considered *unclean*. After this, the parents would then follow the order to present their child to the Lord. This means Jesus was about one month old when brought into the temple.

Read Leviticus 12:6-8. What sacrifice was required, and what exception was made?

What did Joseph and Mary offer in Luke 2:24, and what does this tell us about them?

Led by God to the temple that day was another man named Simeon. Luke 2:25 says *"the Holy Spirit was upon him."* This was unusual. In the Old Testament, people were anointed with the Holy Spirit, but only for a specific task. Simeon had the rare gift of having the Spirit with him continually.

What was the role of the Holy Spirit in Simeon's life, according to verses 26–28?

Look up the following verses about the Holy Spirit's role in your life: John 14:26; Acts 1:8; Romans 5:5. What do you learn about the Holy Spirit through God's Word?

The Spirit reveals to Simeon that this infant named Jesus is the long-awaited Messiah. This causes Simeon to break into a hymn of blessing! We know this psalm as the ***Nunc Dimittis***. This is Latin for the first few words of Luke 2:29, and translates as "Now Dismiss." Interestingly, this is the fourth hymn recorded so far in the book of Luke.

What does this tell us about encounters with Jesus? How does Psalm 95:1 and Ephesians 5:19 support this? Do you have a favorite Christmas song about Jesus?

Simeon's words speak straight to the point. Jesus would be a *"light for revelation"* to both Jew and gentile. (Luke 2:32)

What did Jesus say about the *"light"* in John 3:19-21?

Simeon foresaw what it meant for Jesus to be the light. He would reveal hearts. He would cause many to fall or rise. Jesus would be divisive, and that would cause conflict. Tim Keller writes, "The word of Simeon is that Christians should expect and be ready for trouble. They should expect conflict as a way to get to peace. We can see it in Jesus, in how he brought peace through the agony of the cross. We should not be surprised, then, when conflicts come upon us."

One form of conflict is <u>among people</u>. As Keller puts it, "The manger at Christmas means that, if you live like Jesus, there won't be room for you in a lot of inns." How have you seen that to be true?

The other form of conflict is <u>within people</u>. How can repentance and submission sometimes create an "inner conflict"?

Day Twenty-Two

LUKE 2:36-39

┌─ major moment: ─────────────────────────────────────┐

  With Jesus in the temple, Anna gave thanks and prophesied.

└──┘

What kind of person do you hope to be when you are old? Is there someone above you in age who lives well for Christ who can serve as an example for you?

Today we will look into the life of the prophetess, Anna. Luke 2:36 tells us she was advanced in years. Most of the years of her life, she was widowed.

At least how old was Anna when Jesus arrived at the temple that day?

Luke makes a point to show Anna's faithfulness to the Lord. For hundreds of years, there have been no prophets, no word from the Lord. Yet at this critical time in history, God raises up several to prophesy (Zechariah and Simeon), not the least of which is a woman named Anna from the little, forgotten tribe of Asher. God loves to show His greatness through the humble and lowly.

What else do we know about Anna? Fill in the blank from Luke 2:37:

"She did _____ _____

from the _____ ..."

This could mean that she had physical housing on the outside gates, or it could loosely translate, "She never missed a service."

Finish the verse.

"... worshiping with _____ and

*_____ **night and day.** "*

Anna not only honored God visibly in service, but also privately at home in her personal life.

In what ways does Anna live a 1 Thessalonians 5:16-22 life?

Anna shows two inspiring ways that we, as Jesus-followers, should grow as we age.

What is the first thing Anna does in Luke 2:38?

What is the second?

As you age, how are you doing in these two areas?

Day Twenty-Three

MATTHEW 2:1-2

┌─ major moment: ─────────────────────────────────

The wise men came looking for the king of the Jews.

└──

Completely unique to the book of Matthew is a look into the wise men who came to visit Jesus. Our Christmas songs and pageants always depict three kings who arrive at the manger. But let's look at this event from a historical perspective.

Many scholars believe that at least two years passed between Jesus' birth and the wise men's visit. Sometimes the wise men are referred to as "magi" from the Greek word *magoi*. This is where we get our words "magic" and "magician." But the word "magi" really refers to a sage. They were probably students of astrology, a common practice in this time period. They were definitely wealthy men of high standing in society, meaning they were respected both in politics and religion, but they were not necessarily kings. Also notice that nowhere does it say there were three men. For all we know, there could have been 30. And men of this standing, traveling this distance, probably traveled with an entire entourage.

How does the historical perspective differ from what we are accustomed to?

Back in Babylon, which was east of Judea, there remained a large Jewish community from back in the days of exile. It appears these wise men from the east had been influenced by Jewish teachings, as they came looking for a "king of the Jews" by following a star.

In Numbers 22, the king of Moab asks a man from the east named Balaam to come out and curse the people of Israel. Instead, Balaam receives a word from God and pronounces a blessing. Read Numbers 24:17. What would come out of Jacob?

What would rise out of Israel? What might this represent?

_____

The wise men followed a star, looking for a king. They were looking for the one who had been *"born"* king (Matthew 2:2). In other words, He wasn't going to become a king. He was born a king. Also notice the title the wise men give to Jesus right at the beginning of His life: "King of the Jews."

What name was given Jesus at the end of His life, according to Matthew 27:37?

_____

What is the eternal name and title given to Jesus in Revelation 19:16?

_____

The wise men arrived in the capital city of Jerusalem, looking for a King. There was one slight problem with this.

Who does Matthew 2:1 tell us is the king of Judea?

_____

We'll talk more about that king tomorrow.

Day Twenty-Four

---

major moment:

King Herod felt threatened by news of the born Messiah.

Today we will take a look into Herod, the king of Judea. Historically, Herod was given control of the region by the Roman government and ruled from 40 B.C. to A.D. 4. He was an especially violent ruler, killing anyone who threatened his rule. He even murdered his own wife and two of his sons when he felt he couldn't trust them. His rule meant everything to him.

What was Herod's reaction to the wise men's news in Matthew 2:3? Why?

What was his first step in verse 4?

The word "disturbed" or "troubled" more literally translates into "terrified." Feeling terrified, Herod gathered the religious leaders and lawyers of his day. They were educated, intelligent men who could interpret the Scriptures. These men quoted from Micah 5:2 and said the Messiah would be born in Bethlehem. Yet we cannot help but notice the apathy these leaders had to the Word. They did not go in search of the Messiah. They wanted to appear wise.

> David Platt says of the scribes, and of us, "… mere knowledge of the Scriptures is not enough. You can know the text well yet still miss the point." Has this ever felt true for you? How can we guard against this?

Perhaps my favorite insight on this particular passage comes from Tim Keller's book *Hidden Christmas*. Keller writes, "Each of us wants the world to orbit around us and our needs and desires. We do not want to serve God or our neighbor – we want them to serve us. In every heart, then, there is a 'little King Herod' that wants to rule and that is threatened by anything that may compromise its omnipotence and sovereignty. … Why do you think it is so hard to pray? Why do you think it is so hard to concentrate on the most glorious person possible? … In Romans 7:15, Paul says 'What I hate I do.' There is still a little King Herod inside you."

> How does Romans 3:10-11 and Romans 8:7-8 support this?

How can we fight the "little King Herod" inside of us? (Psalm 119:9; Philippians 2:3)

Herod sent the wise men out with lies about his desire to also worship the new king. (Matthew 2:8) But his secret meeting and his question about the star's timing showed he was already plotting murder in his mind. He then covered his sin by trying to appear holy. As Matthew Henry puts it, "The greatest wickedness often conceals itself under a mask of piety."

As we have learned from Herod and the religious leaders, we have a heart condition. How does Matthew 15:8 describe it?

What does Psalm 51:10 encourage us to pray?

Day Twenty-Five

MATTHEW 2:9-10

---

major moment:

The star guided the wise men to Jesus.

When the wise men first saw the star in Matthew 2:2, they simply said *"it rose."*
Using the little information they had, they set out toward the most obvious place you
would expect to find the ***"king of the Jews."*** Jerusalem was the capital city and held
the palace. But the King they sought was not there. After visiting with king Herod,
the wise men followed his advice to head toward Bethlehem. The town of Bethlehem
was approximately six miles south of Jerusalem. These men stepped out in faith and
start heading south.

When they first saw the star back at home, it was simply a sign in the sky.
What supernatural event takes place in Matthew 2:9?

What similar event took place in Exodus 13:21?

God used a still star in the sky, He used the wise men's own knowledge, He used an evil king and He used a supernatural event, all to guide these men toward Jesus. What does God promise you in Psalm 32:8?

Matthew Henry wrote, *"We should be glad of every thing that will show us the way to Christ."* Indeed, this was the reaction of the wise men.

Fill in the blanks from Matthew 2:10:

"When they saw the star, they _____

_____ *with* _____ _____*."*

Fill in the blanks from Psalm 105:3:

"Glory in his holy name; let the _____ *of those who*

_____ *the* _____ _____*!"*

What does this teach us about seeking Jesus?

_____

The wise men were guided by a star to the place where they would find Jesus. You might say we are still being guided by a star today.

Read Revelation 22:16. What star guides us now?

_____

weekend reflections + prayer

The very last word that we read this week was *"joy"* (Matthew 2:10). We have seen joy throughout our readings. Simeon had joy when he held the baby Messiah in His arms. Anna had joy as she gave thanks and prophesied. The wise men had joy as they began to realize their long journey was not in vain. A star was literally lighting their way! But not everyone had joy, did they? Herod felt threatened and *"troubled"* (Matthew 2:3), not joyful. Consequently, he sent the wise men to see this newborn king, while he stayed back.

Joy does not just happen to us. It is not dependent on our outward circumstances. Joy is a condition of the heart. Joy is peace and hope despite circumstances. And these moments of history remind us of the only source of joy in life. **Christmas points out that joy is only found in Jesus.**

Do you have joy? Christmas is a busy time of year, but then, isn't that the case most of the year? We chase many things. We do more and more. Yet sometimes, we don't understand why we are missing joy. Joy isn't found in doing. It isn't found in "good moments" or the perfect day. Joy is found when our hearts are at rest in the one who came as a baby in a manger to save us.

It is a choice we must make every day — to choose joy. Will we seek Him, thank Him, hold on to Him? Or will we push Him away? Jesus is joy. If we want joy, we should choose Jesus.

---

prayer:

Father God, I confess that I try to fill my heart with temporary things. I want perfect moments, and I feel pressure to do more and be more. But that does not bring me joy, Father. Only Jesus brings joy. So, I sit in Your presence today. Fill my heart with You. And may the joy You pour into me overflow on everything and everyone around me. In Jesus' name, amen.

week six

Love

Christmas is a look into the depths of God's love.

Day Twenty-Six

MATTHEW 2:11-12

---

major moment:

The wise men worshipped Jesus and brought Him gifts.

The wise men had left their homeland in the far east to search for a newborn king in Judea. Naturally, they first went to the palace. But the King was not there.

Where did the wise men find the King they were searching for? (Matthew 2:11)

We have learned through this study that Mary and Joseph were quite poor. Imagine the situation the wise men find, in Mary and Joseph's house, at the end of the star. They had traveled for months to find a King. This situation could have caused them to miss the miracle before them.

Can you think of a time that you almost missed seeing God's goodness and blessings because it didn't look like you expected?

Matthew 2:11 is an important verse because it is a fulfillment of Old Testament prophecy.

What does Psalm 72:10-11 say of the Messiah?

What does Isaiah 60:6 say of the Messiah?

These wise men from far away nations fell down and worshipped a small child in a humble home. They were looking for the "King of the Jews," but Jesus was more than that. Jesus would be the King of all nations.

Philippians 2:10-11 says that everyone, in heaven, on earth and under the earth, shall someday do what?

It was customary in the east to bring gifts when visiting a king. While the wise men probably had no knowledge of the significance, scholars agree that there is symbolism in each of the three gifts given.

Gold represented royalty. It was found in palaces and with kings. (2 Kings 5:5) Why was this fitting for Jesus?

Frankincense represented God. It was an incense that was only to be used for God in Jewish temple worship. (Exodus 30:34-38) Why was this fitting for Jesus?

You might say myrrh represents humanity. It was a spice used for embalming a person after they had died. Read John 19:39-40 and write down how the myrrh was used. What does this remind us about Jesus?

Our reaction to Jesus should be similar to the wise men. Coming before our King should cause us to bow down and worship Him. And while there is no gift worthy of Him, and nothing that can "buy" us His favor, there is something we can offer Him in love and gratitude every day.

According to Romans 12:1, what gift can we offer Jesus? What does this mean?

Day Twenty-Seven

MATTHEW 2:13-15

┌─ **major moment:** ─────────────────────────┐

Jesus' family fled to Egypt, and like Israel's past, there would be a new exodus.

└──┘

In today's reading, we learn that Joseph must have taken his family and fled to Egypt. Egypt was approximately 90 miles from Bethlehem. History tells us that in the Egyptian city of Alexandria, there was a large Jewish community of people who had fled because of trouble with King Herod. Perhaps this is where Jesus' family settled. Jesus, God's own Son, was a refugee.

However, today's reading is about so much more than a family on the run. Remember, Matthew was a Jewish man writing to a mostly Jewish audience. This audience would have been extremely familiar with their history. Through the rest of Chapter 2, **Matthew shows how Jesus is the perfect fulfillment of Israel's past.** Let's dive into some history!

Straight away, while not explicit, Matthew implies an important link between Jesus and history.

- According to Matthew 2:13, 16, what was Herod's intention?
- Look back in time to Exodus 1:22. What was the pharaoh's intention?
- Just as Jesus was saved from Herod, one child was saved from Pharaoh's plan. Who? (Exodus 2:10)

Matthew says that Jesus' journey to (and out of) Egypt was to fulfill the words of the prophet found in Hosea 11:1.

Fill in the blanks from Hosea 11:1

"Out of _____ I called _____

_____."

In this particular verse, Hosea referenced God leading His people out of Egypt and the slavery they were in. But before Pharaoh would release God's people, there had to be a series of plagues.

What would rise out of Israel? What might this represent? (Numbers 24:17)

What was the final plague that led to Israel's release? (Exodus 12:29)

How was Israel kept safe from this? (Exodus 12:3, 7, 13)

This event, celebrated even to this day by those of Jewish faith, became known as the Passover. According to 1 Corinthians 5:7, what is Jesus?

Jesus coming out of Egypt was symbolic of God's people coming out of Egypt thousands of years earlier. As Platt says it, "Jesus inaugurates the new exodus." God was once again bringing His people, particularly His Son, out of Egypt. The blood of the Lamb would once again save. God had saved His people from Egyptian slavery in the past, but now He would save us from another slavery.

According to Matthew 1:21, what slavery would Jesus save us from?

Day Twenty-Eight

MATTHEW 2:16-18

> **major moment:**
>
> ## Herod killed children in Bethlehem, and like Israel's past, mothers wept for their children.

Herod was a particularly violent ruler. Especially toward the end of his reign, we know through historical accounts that he killed anyone he felt might threaten his power. In today's reading, we see his violence extended even toward innocent children. Based on the population of villages like Bethlehem, we can assume that somewhere between 10-20 boys under the age of two would have been killed. What anguish and pain for the families of Bethlehem!

Matthew records this particular event to link it to the words of the prophet Jeremiah found in Jeremiah 31:15. Jeremiah was writing to the people of Israel, telling them of the coming pain they would endure because of the exile by Babylon. This was another major moment in Israel's past.

Yet most importantly, Jeremiah's words do not end with Jeremiah 31:15 and weeping.

Read Jeremiah 31:16-17. Then fill in the blank for verse 17:

"There is _____ *for your*

_____, *declares the Lord."*

This hope was Jesus. In the midst of Israel's painful exile, Jeremiah had promised hope. In the midst of Bethlehem's painful loss, Jesus was the hope. In this life, we, too, will have pain. But there can be hope in the midst of it. Write down what you learn about suffering and hope from the following verses.

Isaiah 43:2-4

2 Corinthians 4:8-10

2 Corinthians 4:16-18

Jeremiah 31 is a particularly important chapter because in it is mentioned the *"new covenant."* **Read Jeremiah 31:31-34.**

What would be different in the new covenant? (v. 34)

The old covenant required continual animal sacrifices to try and cover sin.
What does Jesus say of the new covenant in Luke 22:20 and Matthew 26:28?

Day Twenty-Nine

MATTHEW 2:19-23

— major moment:

Jesus' family returned to Nazareth, and like
Israel's prophets of the past, He would be rejected.

When King Herod died, his son, Archelaus, took over. Archelaus was known as a cruel and violent ruler and was so hated by the Jews that Caesar Augustus eventually removed him for mismanagement and banished him to Gaul (Gaul was a large, remote area north of Rome which included present-day France). No wonder Joseph was hesitant to go back toward this evil ruler!

Yet the angel told him to return to the land of Israel, specifically to Nazareth. This was where Matthew will once again pick up the parallel between Jesus and Israel's past. Matthew says that the prophets' words were fulfilled when Jesus became a Nazarene. However, there was no direct quote from a prophet saying the Messiah would be from Nazareth. So what was Matthew's meaning? Let's take a look.

According to Luke 6:22–23, how were Israel's prophets of the past treated?

Yet even more important than identifying with the prophets was the predicted treatment of the coming Messiah. What did Isaiah 53:3 say about how the Messiah would be treated?

Nazareth was a small, poor town in the middle of nowhere, and historically, it was known to have gentiles living there as well — something many Jewish communities considered a disgrace. Read John 1:46. What can we gather was the common consensus regarding Nazareth?

Being from Nazareth meant being looked down on. Even from the beginning, Jesus was set up to be despised and rejected. And honestly, have we treated Him much better? In his commentary on Matthew, David Platt writes, "The reality is that in our minds and in our hearts, we have all rejected Him. This is the core of what it means to be a sinner, and this is precisely whom Jesus came to save."

Read 1 John 3:1. Because of God's love, we are called what?

Now read Romans 5:8-11 to see how this is possible.

Jesus faced rejection, a rejection that led to His death, all so we could have acceptance.

Write a prayer, thanking Jesus that His rejection is your acceptance, and His death is your eternal life.

Day Thirty

---
major moment:

Jesus grew up and had the grace of God upon Him.

A baby was born, far from his home, and laid in a feeding trough. Angels announced His birth. Both poor shepherds and wealthy sages came to visit Him. A jealous king tried to kill Him. I'm going to go out on a limb and say this is unlike your birth story.

Yet Jesus **was** like you and me. His experience was that of an ordinary human child. Even though He was God, He also took on the fullness of humanity.

Fill in the blanks for the first part of Luke 2:40:

"And the child _____ and became

_____, filled with _____."

Jesus had to grow up. He had to learn to walk and talk. He would have outgrown His sandals year after year and scraped His knees playing games. He would have gotten hungry and tired and needed a nap. He even had to learn to read and write ... the God whose very Word created the universe!

Even though Jesus was God, He took on the form of a man. (Philippians 2:6-7)
According to Hebrews 2:14-18, why did He have to become a man?

Hebrews 4:15 reminds us that because Jesus Christ became human, He is able to sympathize with our what?

Jesus was like us in humanity. He "grew up." This is similar to what Luke says about John in Luke 1:80. Yet, there was something different about Jesus.

Fill in the blanks for the ending to Luke 2:40 (Here I have used NIV).

"And the _____ of

_____ was on him."

Jesus had the grace of God upon Him. It was not just with Him, but **inside** of Him. And because God came in human form, was born in a wooden manger, and hung to die on a wooden cross, He now offers that same gift of grace to us.

According to John 14:20, who did Jesus say would be in us?

And according to verse 26, in what form would He be in us?

Isn't that what it's all about? This baby born in a manger came so He could fulfill the righteous life we could not, experience full humanity and then die. But through His death, His Spirit can now live in us. Jesus took care of the sin that separated us so we can be with Him forever. We, too, can receive the *"favor of God"* (Luke 2:40).

Write a prayer thanking God for the gift of His Spirit and the gift of His Son.

weekend reflections + prayer

Have you sensed the love of God this week? The wise men may have given expensive gifts, but God's love is an incomparable gift. Out of love, God gave us prophecies in the Old Testament, so we could recognize His Son when He came. Out of love, God introduced His Son to us as both fully God and fully human. Being God, He was perfect. Being human, He could die. In His love, Jesus did die. He died to set us free from sin and death. And when He rose back to life again on the third day, His love calls out that we, too, can have life! Eternal life. Life with Him.

Do you want to see God's love for you? Look at the baby lying in a manger. He preserved the exact right family lines for generations. He miraculously sent a forerunner. He guided a Roman emperor. When the inns were overfilled, He saved a place among the animals. He created the tree the manger came from. He grew the grass for the hay. He designed the shepherds and sages, the devout man and the dutiful prophetess, all who sought a glimpse of Him. He even accounted for the very scribes who ignored Him, and the king who tried to kill Him. And He did it all for you. **Christmas is a look into the depths of God's love.**

Fix your eyes today on the one who was born, and who died, and who rose back to life. Be in awe that His love did this for you.

prayer:

Father, we are humbled today. How great is Your love for us! Christmas has reminded us of its depths. You sent Your Son for us. There is no greater love. I pray the words of Paul in Ephesians 3:18. Help us to comprehend the breadth and length and height and depth of Your love. I know Your love surpasses knowledge, but give us a glimpse today. In Jesus' name, amen.

Works Cited

1. Anyabwile, Thabiti. Exalting Jesus in Luke. Christ-Centered Exposition Commentary, edited by David Platt, Daniel L. Akin and Tony Merida. Nashville, TN: Holman, 2018.

2. Bock, Darrell L. Luke 1:1 - 9:50. Baker Exegetical Commentary on the New Testament, edited by Robert W. Yarbrough and Joshua W. Jipp. Grand Rapids, MI: Baker Academic, 1994.

3. Henry, M. Matthew Henry's Commentary on the Whole Bible: Complete and Unabridged in one olume. Peabody: Hendrickson, 1994.

4. Keller, Timothy. Hidden Christmas. New York, NY: Penguin, 2016.

5. Lewis, C.S. Miracles. New York: Macmillan, 1947.

6. Platt, David. Exalting Jesus in Matthew. Christ-Centered Exposition Commentary, edited by David Platt, Daniel L. Akin and Tony Merida. Nashville, TN: Holman, 2013.

7. Ryle, J.C. Expository Thoughts on the Gospels: Luke, vol. 1. Carlisle, PA: Banner of Truth, 2012.

8. Warren, Pastor Rick. What Gives Me Hope. Facebook, 29 Oct. 2015, 3:00 p.m., https://www.facebook.com/pastorrickwarren/posts/10153665628940903:0. Accessed 15 June. 2020.

Reflect on...

As we end our study, let's marvel once again at how God has delighted in pointing us to His Son! He gave us the Old Testament prophets and a man named John to prepare the way. He sent a star and angels. He delivered the news to old men and women, as well as young. Wealthy men from afar spread the word, in addition to lowly, local shepherds. Not everyone believed or received the news. But the message was loud and clear: **"A Savior has been born to you. He is the Messiah!"**

But as we end, I can't help but ask, "Why?" Why did God go to the trouble? Why be born into this messy, painful world?

I want to leave you with this quote I came across when I first began researching this study. It has stood out in my mind ever since. I find it to be the perfect description of what Christmas really means. He was born, so He could die ... for you. You are that precious to Him.

Merry Christmas, friend,

FROM ALL OF US AT FIRST 5!

"In the Christian story God...

comes down; down from the heights of absolute being into time and space, down into humanity; down further still, if embryologists are right, to recapitulate in the womb ancient and pre-human phases of life ... down to the very roots and seabed of the Nature He has created. But He goes down to come up again and bring the whole ruined world up with Him ... [O]ne may think of a diver, first reducing himself to nakedness, then glancing in mid-air, then gone with a splash, vanished, rushing down through green and warm water into black and cold water, down through increasing pressure into the death-like region of ooze and slime and old decay; then up again, back to color and light, his lungs almost bursting, till suddenly he breaks surface again, holding in his hand the dripping, precious thing that he went down to recover."

- C.S. LEWIS, MIRACLES

"But to all who did receive him, who believed in his name, he gave the right to become children of God."

John 1:12

Notes

Notes

About Proverbs 31 Ministries

**She is clothed with strength and dignity;
she can laugh at the days to come.**

PROVERBS 31:25

Proverbs 31 Ministries is a nondenominational, nonprofit Christian ministry that seeks to lead women into a personal relationship with Christ. With Proverbs 31:10-31 as a guide, Proverbs 31 Ministries reaches women in the middle of their busy days through free devotions, podcast episodes, speaking events, conferences, resources, online Bible studies and training in the call to write, speak and lead others.

We are real women offering real-life solutions to those striving to maintain life's balance, in spite of today's hectic pace and cultural pull away from godly principles.

Wherever a woman may be on her spiritual journey, Proverbs 31 Ministries exists to be a trusted friend who understands the challenges she faces and walks by her side, encouraging her as she walks toward the heart of God.

Visit us online today at proverbs31.org!

Proverbs 31
MINISTRIES